Hawaii

by Patricia K. Kummer,
the Capstone Press Geography Department

Content Consultant:
Donne Florence
Public Information Officer
University of Hawaii

CAPSTONE PRESS
MANKATO, MINNESOTA

CAPSTONE PRESS

818 North Willow Street • Mankato, MN 56001
http://www.capstone-press.com

Printed in the United States of America.

Library of Congress Cataloging-in-Publication Data
Kummer, Patricia K.
    Hawaii/by Patricia K. Kummer.
    p. cm.--(One nation)
    Includes bibliographical references and index.
    Summary: Gives an overview of the state of Hawaii, including its history, geography, people, and living conditions.
    ISBN 1-56065-525-9
    1. Hawaii--Juvenile literature. [1. Hawaii.]
    I. Title. II. Series.
DU623.K96 1998
996.9--dc21

                                          97-7070
                                            CIP
                                            AC

Photo credits
Michele Burgess, 20, 34
Capstone Press, 4 (left)
Gerald D. Carr, 5 (right)
Ron Colbroth, 33
William B. Folsom, 29
FPG/Mark Scott, 6
Hawaii Visitors Bureau, 4 (right), Lyon Arboretum, 5 (left)
International Stock/Richard Pharaoh, cover; Michael Howell, 12
Maui Visitors Bureau/Jack Hollingsworth, 8
Chuck Place, 10, 30
Root Resources/Bill Glass, 16
James P. Rowan, 22
Lynn Seldon, 18
Kay Shaw, 25, 26

Table of Contents

Fast Facts about Hawaii

State Flag

Location: In the north central Pacific Ocean
Size: 6,425 square miles (16,705 square kilometers)

Population: 1,186,815 (1995 United States Census Bureau figures)
Capital: Honolulu
Date admitted to the Union: August 21, 1959; the 50th state

Nene (Hawaiian goose)

Largest cities:
Honolulu, Hilo,
Kailua, Kaneohe,
Waipahu, Pearl City,
Waimalu,
Mililani Town,
Schofield Barracks,
Wahiawa

Nickname: The Aloha
State

Yellow hibiscus

State bird: Nene
(Hawaiian goose)
State flower: Yellow
hibiscus
State tree: Kukui
(candlenut)
State song: "Hawaii
Ponoi" ("Our Own
Hawaii") by King
Kalakaua and Henry
Berger

Kukui (candlenut)

Chapter 1
The Aloha State

Hawaii is known for its aloha (ah-LOH-hah) spirit. This is the friendly welcome given to newcomers by people from Hawaii.

Aloha is a Native Hawaiian word. It stands for love, greetings, and kindness. Today, people from Hawaii use the word to say hello and goodbye.

Native Hawaiians are people whose families lived in Hawaii before the arrival of Asians or Europeans. They share the islands with those who have moved there.

Leis, Luaus, and the Hula

People in Hawaii practice many Native Hawaiian customs. They welcome guests with leis (LAYS).

People in Hawaii welcome visitors with leis.

Hawaiian feasts called luaus are popular in Hawaii.

Leis are necklaces that are usually made of Hawaiian flowers. Some leis are also made of feathers or shells.

Luaus (LU-ows) are Native Hawaiian feasts. People eat a pig that was roasted in an underground oven. Another luau food is poi (POY). This is made by pounding taro root into a paste. Taro root is the root of an herb that people can eat. Many people use their fingers to scoop poi from a dish.

Most luaus include dancing and music. The hula (HOO-lah) is a special Hawaiian dance that tells a story. The word hula means dance in Hawaiian. Women and men move their hands, arms, hips, and feet to music. Each movement helps tell the story. Hula dancers spend years learning their craft.

Surfing

Surfing began in Hawaii. Early Hawaiians held surfing competitions. They surfed on heavy boards made of koa wood. Koa wood is from a Hawaiian tree.

Oahu's North Shore has the world's best surfing beaches. Hawaii hosts the world surfing championships there each November and December. The waves are at their largest during these months.

Aloha Stadium

Aloha Stadium is in Honolulu. Each year this stadium hosts three bowl games. On Christmas Day, two college football teams play in the Aloha Bowl. In January, college all-stars play in the Hula Bowl. Hula dancers perform at halftime. The Pro Bowl is usually played at Aloha Stadium in January. The best professional players compete in the Pro Bowl.

Chapter 2
The Land

Hawaii is the only U.S. state not in North America. It lies in the north central Pacific Ocean. It is 2,091 miles (3,346 kilometers) southwest of San Francisco, California. Hawaii is the southernmost part of the United States.

Hawaii is also the nation's only island state. It is made up of 132 islands. Only eight of the islands are large. People live on seven of them. They are Hawaii, Maui, Lanai, Molokai, Oahu, Kauai, and Niihau. The eighth large island is Kahoolawe. No one lives there. It was used as a bombing target by the U.S. military.

The island of Hawaii is the largest island. The state is named after this island. People call the

Hawaii is an island state in the Pacific Ocean. It is covered with waterfalls and lush, green plants.

Waikiki is Hawaii's most famous beach.

island of Hawaii the Big Island. This is so people do not confuse the island and the state.

Volcanic Mountains

Underground volcanoes formed Hawaii's islands. Over many years, lava mountains pushed up from the ocean. They are Hawaii's mountains today.

Mauna Kea is a dormant volcano on the Big Island. Dormant means not active. Mauna Kea has not erupted in 4,000 years. Mauna Kea is also the state's highest point. It rises 13,796 feet (4,139 meters) above sea level.

The Big Island also has two active volcanoes. Kilauea has been erupting since 1983. Mauna Loa last erupted in 1984. These volcanoes are in Hawaii Volcanoes National Park.

Coastline and Beaches

Hawaii's total coastline is 1,052 miles (1,683 kilometers) long. Rugged lava cliffs stand on parts of the coast.

White sand beaches line much of the coast. One of the most famous Hawaiian beaches is Waikiki. It is on Oahu. Green sand and black sand beaches are on the Big Island. Crushed lava from volcano eruptions formed them.

Valleys, Rain Forests, and Deserts

Valleys lie between the state's mountains. Taro grows near streams in the valleys. Sheep and cattle graze there, too.

The Largest Islands

Hawaii	hah-WHY-ee
Maui	MOW-ee
Lanai	lah-NAH-ee
Molokai	moh-loh-KAH-ee
Oahu	oh-AH-hoo
Kauai	kah-WAH-ee
Niihau	NEE-ee-how
Kahoolawe	kah-HOH-oh-LAH-vay

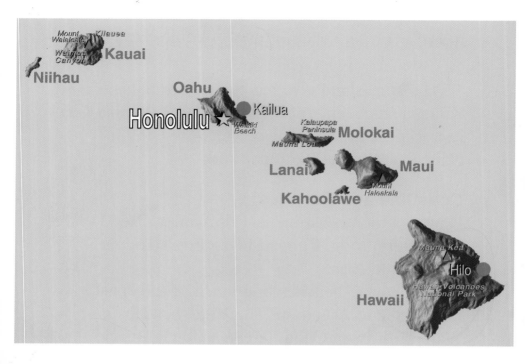

Rain forests cover about 40 percent of the Hawaiian Islands. Lehua, koa, and huge tree ferns grow there.

Some islands have deserts. Garden of the Gods on Lanai is a desert. It has many strangely shaped lava rocks.

Rivers and Waterfalls

Many short rivers and streams flow from Hawaii's mountains. They run into the ocean. Wailuku is one of the state's longest rivers. It is on the Big Island.

Many of the state's streams tumble over waterfalls. Water gathers in pools at the bottom of the waterfalls.

Wildlife

Only seals and small bats were living on Hawaii when people first moved there. This was because it was so far away from any other land. People brought animals with them, and the animal population grew.

Hawaii also has some unique land birds. They include honeycreepers, coots, and nenes. Humpback whales swim in Hawaiian waters.

Climate

Hawaii has mild, sunny weather all year long. Cool winds blow from the northeast. The average temperature is about 75 degrees Fahrenheit (24 degrees Celsius).

Rain falls mainly on the northeast sides of the islands. Mount Waialeale is on Kauai. It is the wettest place on earth. About 460 inches (1,168 centimeters) of rain fall there each year.

Strong windstorms called hurricanes sometimes hit the western sides of the islands. In 1992, Hurricane Iniki caused $2 billion in damages on Kauai.

Chapter 3
The People

People who live in Hawaii come from many backgrounds. They have Polynesian, Asian, and European backgrounds. Others are African American. They come from the mainland United States. The mainland United States are 48 states that border one another in North America.

Intermarriage in Hawaii is common. Intermarriage means marriage between people of different ethnic groups. About 60 percent of children have mixed ethnic backgrounds.

Almost 90 percent of the people live in or near Hawaii's cities. About 75 percent of them live in cities on Oahu. This island has nine of Hawaii's 10 largest cities.

About 75 percent of Hawaii residents live on Oahu.

About 62 percent of Hawaii's residents are Asian Americans.

Asian Americans

About 62 percent of the people in Hawaii are
Asian Americans. Hawaii has the nation's largest
percentage of Asian Americans. Most of them
have Japanese, Filipino, Chinese, or Korean
backgrounds.

People from Asia first arrived between the
1850s and 1920s. They worked on Hawaii's
sugarcane and pineapple plantations. A plantation
is a large farm. Asians in Hawaii left the
plantations and opened shops and restaurants.

Today, Chinese Americans are some of Hawaii's leading businesspeople. Japanese Americans hold about half of Hawaii's government offices.

White Residents of Hawaii

About 33 percent of Hawaii's residents are white. A resident is someone who lives in a particular place. Hawaii has the smallest percentage of white people of any state.

The families of many white people arrived in Hawaii in the 1800s. Many of them were missionaries or plantation owners from the United States. Businesspeople came from England and Germany. Many Scottish and Portuguese people became plantation managers.

Whites still come from the mainland United States. Some take jobs in new Hawaii businesses. Others retire in Hawaii.

Native Hawaiians

About 9 percent of the people are Native Hawaiians. Their families were Hawaii's first people. They came from Polynesian islands in the

Pacific Ocean. Because of intermarriage, only about 1,000 people are 100 percent Native Hawaiian.

Oahu has the largest number of Native Hawaiians. Native Hawaiians make up almost half of Molokai's population. About 250 Native Hawaiians live on Niihau. They make up 95 percent of that island's population. They speak the Hawaiian language. The Hawaiian language has only 13 letters.

In recent years, Native Hawaiians have worked to become more active in government. Hawaiian is now one of Hawaii's official languages. In 1986, Hawaii elected its first Native-Hawaiian governor.

Other Ethnic Groups

About 7 percent of island residents are Hispanic Americans. One-third of them are Puerto Ricans. Many of their families arrived in the early 1900s. Only 2 percent of the people in the state are African American.

Native Hawaiians make up about 9 percent of Hawaii's population. Their families were Hawaii's first people.

Chapter 4
Hawaii History

Hawaii's first people were Polynesians. They arrived about 1,700 years ago. They sailed from the Marquesas Islands in huge canoes. Later, other Polynesians came from Tahiti.

Polynesians brought sugarcane, banana, and taro plants. They raised chickens and pigs. They built ponds for catching fish.

These first Hawaiians believed in many gods. For example, Pele was the goddess of the volcanoes. She lived in Kilauea Volcano on the Big Island and was said to cause the volcano to erupt.

Hawaii's first people were Polynesians. They brought plants and animals and settled on the islands.

The Kingdom of Hawaii

In the 1700s, several chiefs ruled the islands. Kamehameha I (kah-MAY-hah-MAY-hah) was a chief from the Big Island. He won battles on the other islands.

By 1810, Kamehameha had brought the people of the main islands together. He formed the Kingdom of Hawaii. The Kingdom of Hawaii was in place until the end of the 1800s.

Europeans and U.S. Settlers Arrive

English Captain James Cook was the first European to explore Hawaii. He landed on Kauai in 1778 and visited the islands of Niihau, Maui, and Hawaii. In 1779, Cook was killed on the Big Island.

In the 1780s, European and U.S. trading ships arrived. Hawaii became a stopping point on the way to Asia.

Changes Come to Hawaii

In 1820, missionaries from the United States landed on the island of Hawaii. They converted many Hawaiians to Christianity. The missionaries made Hawaiian women wear long dresses called muumuus (MOO-moos). Wearing leis and dancing the hula were discouraged.

Kamehameha was a chief on the Big Island in the 1700s.

U.S. and European whaling ships stopped at Hawaiian ports. Some sailors stayed in Hawaii.

In 1835, a U.S. company started a sugarcane plantation on Kauai. By the 1890s, other U.S. settlers and Europeans had started pineapple plantations.

These plantations needed many workers. Thousands came from China, Japan, Korea, and the Philippines. Asian workers soon outnumbered Native Hawaiians.

LANI E"   LILI'UOKALAN

The Republic of Hawaii

Little by little, U.S. and European planters gained control of Hawaii. They bought much of the land. They changed the laws for their benefit. They also were elected to government offices.

In 1891, Hawaii's only ruling queen came into power. Liliuokalani (lee-LEE-oo-oh-kah-LAH-nee) tried to change the laws. She wanted to return the power to the throne and take it from the planters.

U.S. citizens and Europeans overthrew the queen in 1893. They set up the Republic of Hawaii. A republic is a country with elected officials.

The United States Gains Hawaii

In 1898, the United States annexed Hawaii. Annex means to take control of another country. Two years later, Hawaii became a U.S. territory. A territory is land with its own government but that is owned by another country. People from Hawaii became citizens of the United States.

The United States built many military bases on Oahu. In 1908, it built the naval base at Pearl Harbor. During World War I (1914-1918), Pearl Harbor became a seaplane base. Thousands of Hawaii's citizens fought for the United States in World War I.

Liliuokalani was Hawaii's only ruling queen.

World War II

World War II started in 1939. The United States tried to stay out of the war. Then on December 7, 1941, Japanese planes bombed Pearl Harbor. The next day, the United States declared war on Japan. During the war, 400,000 soldiers and sailors were stationed in Hawaii.

More than 140,000 Hawaii residents were Japanese Americans. Some people feared that Hawaii's Japanese Americans would help Japan. This did not happen. About 4,300 became soldiers in the U.S. Army. They helped the United States win the war in 1945.

The 50th State

In 1959, Hawaii became the 50th state. Hawaii has changed since statehood. The state's population has almost doubled. Sugar and pineapple production has greatly decreased.

Now, tourism is the leading business. To build roads and resorts, people cut down many trees. They also filled in wetlands. This hurt Hawaii's land and wildlife. The people are now working to protect the state's land.

The Japanese bombed the U.S. naval base at Pearl Harbor during World War II.

Native Hawaiians are trying to regain land lost in 1893 and 1898 when the United States took over. Many Native Hawaiians would like to have their own government.

Hawaii's government is trying to solve these problems. It wants a united Hawaii. Hawaii is also looking to become the Health State. The state wants to be a leader in the medical field in the Pacific.

Chapter 5
Hawaii Business

Service industries employ almost 90 percent of Hawaii's workers. These businesses include tourism, real estate, government, and trade. Manufacturing, agriculture, and fishing are other Hawaii businesses.

Tourism

Tourism is Hawaii's leading business. About 7 million people visit Hawaii each year. Many come from the mainland United States. Others travel from Japan and Australia.

Tourists spend about $9 billion in Hawaii each year. Hotels and resorts take in most of this money.

Tourism is Hawaii's leading business. About 7 million people visit Hawaii each year.

Real Estate and the Military

In recent years, many hotels have been built for tourists. More tourists have bought condominiums. They use them as second homes or retirement homes.

Several U.S. military bases are on Oahu. Pearl Harbor is still an important naval base there. The Big Island has a large training base.

Manufacturing and Trade

Pineapple and refined sugar are Hawaii's leading manufactured goods. Clothing and books are also made in Hawaii. Oahu has an oil refinery.

Trade is important to Hawaii. Japan buys caps, T-shirts, and macadamia nuts from the state. Foods are shipped to the mainland United States.

Other food and manufactured goods come from the mainland United States. Hawaii also receives oil from Indonesia.

Agriculture and Fishing

In the past, sugarcane and pineapples were Hawaii's most valuable crops. Today, Hawaii is looking for new crops to grow. They are trying out new fruits and vegetables. They grow coffee

Hawaii has many sugarcane fields. Refined sugar is one of the state's leading manufactured goods.

and macadamia nuts. Guavas and papayas grow on Kauai. The Big Island is known for its popular Kona coffee.

Niihau, Molokai, and the Big Island have cattle ranches. Sheep, hogs, and chickens are raised throughout the islands.

Yellowfin tuna is Hawaii's leading seafood product. Hawaii produces many prawns. Prawns are like shrimp. They are raised in ponds.

Chapter 6
Seeing the Sights

Hawaii is a beautiful and exciting state to visit. Sunbathers and surfers enjoy its beaches. Hikers find waterfalls in the rain forests. Hawaii's museums and palaces tell the state's history.

Oahu, the Gathering Place

Oahu is called the Gathering Place. About 80 percent of Hawaii's people live there. Most tourists start their Hawaiian vacation in Honolulu on Oahu. They take planes or cruise ships to the other islands.

The state capitol building is in Honolulu. It is designed to represent the volcanoes that created the islands. Its pillars look like palm trees. Iolani Palace is also in Honolulu. Hawaii has the nation's only royal palace.

Waimea Canyon is called the Grand Canyon of the Pacific.

The beaches of Waikiki are east of Honolulu. Visitors can learn how to surf. Pearl Harbor is west of Honolulu. The USS *Arizona* Memorial is there. It honors sailors killed during Japan's attack in 1941.

The Polynesian Cultural Center is in far northern Oahu. Seven Polynesian villages have been recreated there. People from different Polynesian groups show their arts and crafts.

Kauai, the Garden Island

Kauai is northwest of Oahu. Rain forests, waterfalls, and canyons cover this island. Wailua Falls is in eastern Kauai. Its two waterfalls drop 80 feet (24 meters).

Waimea Canyon is in western Kauai. It is called the Grand Canyon of the Pacific. The canyon is made out of volcanic rock.

The Spouting Horn is at Kauai's southern tip. Ocean water rushes out of this lava tube and shoots into the air.

Niihau, the Forbidden Island

Niihau is west of Kauai. It is a private island. Only invited guests may stay there.

The Robinson family owns Niihau. They run a cattle and sheep ranch. A relative bought Niihau from King Kamehameha V in 1864. People on Niihau still speak Hawaiian.

Molokai, the Friendly Island

Molokai is east of Oahu. The island's wide-open spaces give visitors room to roam.

Papohaku Beach is in West Molokai. This is Hawaii's largest white sand beach. Puu O Hoku ranch is in East Molokai. Visitors can drive through the ranch and see horses and cattle.

Kalaupapa Peninsula is in northern Molokai. A peninsula is land surrounded on three sides with water. People with Hansen's disease were sent there in 1866. Back then, they were called lepers, and the disease was called leprosy. The disease attacks the skin, nerves, and muscles. Today, about 100 people live there. They are providing treatment or being treated for Hansen's disease.

Lanai, the Pineapple Island

Lanai is south of Molokai. A company called Castle and Cooke now owns most of Lanai. This company has built two luxury resorts. They are near Lanai City. This city is in the middle of the island.

The Luahiwa Petroglyphs are south of Lanai City. Ancient Hawaiians carved pictures into rocks there.

Kahoolawe, the Uninhabited Island

Kahoolawe is south of Lanai. No one has lived on Kahoolawe since World War II. This is when the U.S. military began using it for target practice. Recently, the bombing was stopped, and the island was given back to the people.

Kahoolawe will need to be cleaned up. Then, Hawaiians will be able to visit the graves of relatives who are buried there. Some people may choose to live there in the future.

Maui, the Valley Island

Maui is east of Kahoolawe and Lanai. It is called the Valley Island. A wide valley stretches across the middle of Maui.

East Maui has the world's largest dormant volcano. This is Mount Haleakala. It is in Haleakala National Park.

Lahaina is in West Maui. This was once a great whaling town. Today, many of the homes and shops look like they did in the 1800s.

Hawaii, the Big Island

Hawaii is southeast of Maui. This is the largest island. Kailua-Kona is in western Hawaii. This city is home to the Hawaiian Islands' first Christian church.

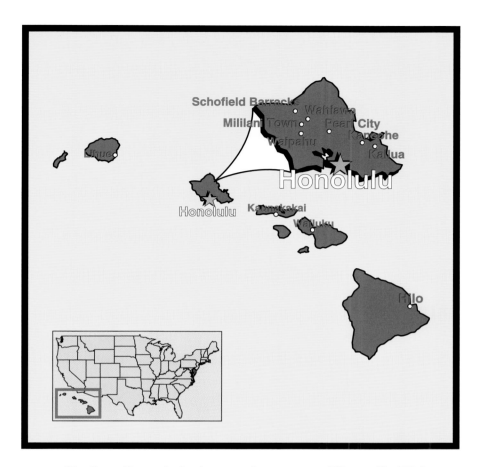

Parker Ranch is in northwestern Hawaii. This is the nation's largest single-owner ranch. It has 50,000 head of cattle.

Hilo is in eastern Hawaii. This is the state's second largest city. Fields of orchids surround the town.

Hawaii Volcanoes National Park is in southeastern Hawaii. Visitors drive there to watch Kilauea erupt.

Hawaii Time Line

A.D. 300-900—Hawaii's first people arrive from Polynesian islands.

1778—English Captain James Cook lands on Kauai and names the islands the Sandwich Islands.

1780s—English, French, and U.S. ships stop to trade in Hawaii.

1792-1810—King Kamehameha I unites the Hawaiian Islands into one kingdom.

1819—King Kamehameha II ends the kapu system. The kapu was a system of laws and consequences.

1820—The first Protestant missionaries arrive in Hawaii from the United States.

1835—A U.S. company starts a sugarcane plantation on Kauai.

1840—King Kamehameha III grants Hawaii its first constitution.

1852—The first Chinese arrive to work on sugarcane plantations.

1868—The first Japanese arrive to work on sugarcane plantations.

1887—King Kalakaua gives the United States sole rights to use Pearl Harbor as a naval base.

1893—U.S. citizens and Europeans overthrow Queen Liliuokalani.

1894—The Republic of Hawaii is established.

1898—The United States annexes Hawaii.

1901—The Hawaiian Pineapple Company, now Dole Pineapple, is founded.

1907—The present-day University of Hawaii is established.

1916—Hawaii Volcanoes National Park and Haleakala National Park are established.

1941—Japan attacks Pearl Harbor and destroys U.S. Navy ships. The bombing causes the United States to enter World War II.

1959—Hawaii becomes the 50th state.

1969—The new state capitol is completed.

1974—The nation's first Japanese-American governor, George Ariyoshi, is elected governor of Hawaii.

1983-1990s—Kilauea Volcano erupts, destroying homes and a town in its path.

1986—John Waihee is elected as the state's first Native-Hawaiian governor.

1991—Carolyn Sapp becomes the first Miss America from Hawaii.

1992—Hurricane Iniki causes four deaths and $2 billion in damages.

1994—Kahoolawe is returned to the state of Hawaii by the U.S. Navy.

1996—Native Hawaiians vote in support of having their own government.

Famous People from Hawaii

Tia Carrere (1967-) Singer and actress who starred in *Wayne's World*; born in Honolulu.

Sanford B. Dole (1844-1926) Lawyer who helped overthrow Queen Liliuokalani (1893); became president of the Republic of Hawaii (1894-1900); born in Honolulu.

Sid Fernandez (1962-) New York Mets pitcher who helped win the World Series (1986); wore the number 50 on his uniform showing he was from the 50th state; born in Honolulu.

Hiram Fong (1906-) First Chinese American elected to the U.S. Senate where he served Hawaii (1959-1977); born in Honolulu.

Mamoru Funai (1932-) Children's writer and illustrator; won awards for *Moke and Poki in the Rain Forest* and *On a Picnic*; born on Kauai.

Clarissa Haili (1901-1979) Famous Native-Hawaiian singer and hula dancer; born in Honolulu.

Daniel Inouye (1924-) World War II war hero; first Japanese American in Congress; served Hawaii in the U.S. House of Representatives (1959-1963) and the Senate (1963-present); born in Honolulu.

Duke Paoa Kahanamoku (1889-1968) Olympic gold medalist for swimming (1912, 1920); known as a champion surfer; born in Haleakala on Maui.

Kamehameha I (1750?-1819) Kingdom of Hawaii's first ruler (1792-1819); joined the Hawaiian Islands (1792-1810); born in Kohala on Hawaii.

Lydia Liliuokalani (1838-1917) Hawaii's last royal ruler (1891-1893); overthrown by U.S. and European business owners; wrote the song "Aloha Oe," Hawaii's song of farewell; born in Honolulu.

Lois Lowry (1937-) Author of *Number the Stars* (1990) and *The Giver* (1994); born in Honolulu.

Bette Midler (1945-) Actress who starred in *Beaches*; Grammy Award-winning singer known for "Wind Beneath My Wings"; born in Honolulu.

Patsy Mink (1927-) Lawyer who served Hawaii in the U.S. House of Representatives (1965-1977, 1990-present); born in Paia on Maui.

Ellison Onizuka (1946-1986) Astronaut who died in the explosion of the space shuttle Challenger; born in Kealakekua on Hawaii.

Chad Rowan (1969-) Sumo wrestler who became the first non-Japanese person to hold the rank of grand champion; born in Waimanalo on Oahu.

Words to Know

annex—to take control of another country

dormant—not active

Hansen's disease—a disease that attacks the skin, nerves, and muscles; once called leprosy

hurricane—a strong windstorm that forms over an ocean and causes great damage when it reaches land

lava—hot liquid that comes from a volcano and hardens as it cools

mainland United States—the 48 states that border one another in North America

missionary—a person sent to do religious or charitable work in a territory or foreign country

plantation—a large farm

rain forest—a forest of many trees where a lot of rain falls

republic—a country with elected officials

territory—an area of land that has its own government but is owned by another country

volcano—a mountain with an opening through which lava erupts

To Learn More

Fradin, Dennis Brindell. *Hawaii*. From Sea to Shining Sea. Chicago: Children's Press, 1994.

Lovett, Sarah. *Kidding Around the Hawaiian Islands*. Santa Fe, N.M.: John Muir Publications, 1990.

Penisten, John. *Honolulu*. Minneapolis: Dillon Press, 1989.

Takaki, Ronald. *Raising Cane: The World of Plantation Hawaii*. New York: Chelsea House, 1994.

Thompson, Kathleen. *Hawaii*. Portrait of America. Austin, Texas: Raintree Steck-Vaughn, 1996.

Useful Addresses

Arizona Memorial and Visitor Center
U.S. Naval Reservation, Pearl Harbor
Honolulu, HI 96818

Haleakala National Park
P.O. Box 369
Makawao, HI 96768

Hulihee Palace
75-5718 Alii Drive
Kailua-Kona, HI 96740

Mauna Loa Macadamia Nut Factory
HC01 Box 3
Hilo, HI 96720

Polynesian Cultural Center
55-370 Kamehameha Highway
Laie, HI 96762

Internet Sites

City.Net Hawaii
http://www.city.net/countries/united_states/hawaii

Travel.org—Hawaii
http://travel.org/hawaii.html

Hawaii State Government
http://www.state.hi.us

Virtual Hawaiian Luau
http://www.si.edu/folklife/vfest/hawaii

Index